Under the Sky of No Complaint

Richard Martin

Lavender Ink
New Orleans
lavenderink.org

Under the Sky of No Complaint

Cover Photo: *Dark Blue Sky with Clouds* by Petr Kratochvil

Author Photo: Nicole Martin

ISBN: 978-1-935084-42-6

A joint publication of:

Lavender Ink
New Orleans
lavenderink.org

Acknowledgements

Some of these poems have appeared in the following publications. Thanks to the editors of:

ACM, Artichoke Haircut, Big Hammer, Brown Box, BURP 8, Chopper 3, Estuaires, Flying Fish, Fell Swoop, Gargoyle, House Organ, LogoDaedulus, Out of Our, and *unarmed.*

The section entitled *Sideways* was first published as a chapbook by Obscure Publications (2004). My thanks to Paul Rosheim, editor and publisher.

The section entitled *Sound Nets* was first published as Unarmed chapbook #6 by *unarmed journal.* My thanks to Michael Mann, editor and publisher.

The section entitled *Strip Meditation* was first published as a chapbook by Igneus Press (2009). My thanks to Peter Kidd, editor and publisher.

Contents

Sideways

Bow of Clean Windows 17
In Just a Few Minutes 18
Sideways 20
Forms of Inspiration 22
Safe 23
Swish 25
And Kiss 26
Statement 29
Sweet Love 31
Decision 33
Go to Oregon 35
Requisition 36
Entertainment 38
Variation on a Field 39
Salutation 40
Tilt 41
Confusion Satori 42
Insight after Dinner at the Diner 43
Roof and Sky 44

Sound Nets

1 51
2 52
3 53
4 54
5 55
6 56

7 57

8 58

9 59

10 60

11 61

12 62

13 63

14 64

Under the Sky of No Complaint

Complete Thought 69

Origin 71

Under the Sky of No Complaint 72

Empty Mailbox 74

I Do 76

The Garden of Upside-Down Trees 78

Subtle Difference 81

After Prosody Class 82

Stoic Surrender 84

Elegy 85

Yellow Tulips 88

Tattered Soliloquy 89

The Pleasure of Noticing 91

Promontory Scrum 92

Spaced Remarks 94

Before Dawn 97

Retroactive 99

Strip Meditation

1 105
2 106
3 107
4 108
5 109
6 110
7 111
8 112
9 113
10 114
11 115
12 117
13 118
14 119

Skylark

In the Bag 123
Ice Cube Cantata 125
Multiple Agendas in the Concept of One 126
Euphoria 127
Syllable Town 129
Mayhem Interlude 130
Closure in a Time of Complaint 132
Thump 133

Talking Heads on Mute 138
Semantic Arteries 139
Fame 140
Bullets 142
Title 144
Slip Up 146
Skylark 147

Under the Sky of No Complaint

And but for the sky there are no fences facin'

—Bob Dylan

for The Binghamton Community Poets

Sideways

Bow of Clean Windows

Living in the ark of my dream
I make another pot of coffee
Rain falls blue into curtains of itself
The animals love Bingo

Once I had some real estate
Could wander in ferns of loneliness
Wait for the birds to change into verbs
On a bed of kisses we tossed

Now the world is weather report
It will snow tonight in the tallest grass
Sirocco of moods followed by deluge
Umbrella sales brisk as wind

I love the bow of clean windows
The unknown port of waiting
Some of the animals snore
Ark traces the path of wet stars

In Just a Few Minutes

I could start with the symbol
Of crows – neighborhood ones, not those
From the pond or the highway –
As the sweater of black wings
I imagine wearing during
A season of lamps – intense
Blue ones, almost sky.
I want to fly.
Or perhaps just the other day –
In search of a transition
A connection for the gaps
In my mind, those holes
You know – that live there
In the mind as place holders
For the bit of metaphysics
Required of everyone
When things – the real objects
Of our lives – make sudden
Nonsense – laugh at us –
Get wavy with their own
Molecular uncertainty – whistle
To us, at us – like they were
Trying to get our attention
About their own loneliness
In the cosmology of being
Here in this setting called
World – I was in Burger King
(Of all places), as if pop-food had
The right – was entitled

To be part of a line – occupy
It with weight & foolishness.
A line now more concerned
With the image of a rainforest –
The canopy of talk – bird lingo
(Symbology again)
In a lingering rain – a rain
That started with intense purpose
& intention, pouring down –
Thundering – until the Amazon
Of the heart, swept into such
A bend of awareness that I
Woke up when handed
A senior coffee (a little cup of joe,
No more than 6 fluid ounces)
By a young, too young employee
Who read the age in my eyes – in my
Thoughts & face & made sure
To not over charge me & be responsible
For getting me wired on something
I could no longer handle
In the sputtering sound of raindrops.

Sideways

Language moves to stillness.
We have the details: old pond
In the ancestor's neighborhood.
Your fear of barns and tall grass.
The snake outside the cabin door
Waiting for grandfather's pitchfork.
Unbelievable stars in black-sneaker night –
False vocabulary for tomorrow.

Can you hear the bongos of narrative
In crystals of world? Flannel clouds, you said
Once. The way the first girlfriend
Required a pasture of kisses.
The train of city arrives.
It squeaks and rumbles.
The keen of electricity sparks whiskey.
Mystery of home and where you're going.

Once a mountain symphony of snowflakes
Beckoned journey. Good friends
You've lost to ice storms. The
People in convenience stores wondering
If you're a misplaced person.
The text of blossoms memorized:
Dogwood, magnolia, rhododendron
In the yard yapping purple.

This is your world and it's OK
To say hello to it.

The salutation of speed runs in your veins.
The polis of remark (how often
We place everything)
Is about love
In and out you go with it.
Name it responsibility or revert to myth.

Worried faces all around you in the brilliant light.
Play with the sun.
It's on your fingertips.
It colors – highlights thought
As thoughts coursing through you.
Make it personal.
Ignored secretaries welcome letters.
Forge gaps into the absence of politics.

Forms of Inspiration

I'm told to write a book
Without clouds or business days.
The characters must be figures sitting
On gold rocks like ailing gods.
All have problems that turn into fish
And bread – useful paraphernalia.

My name is Franz.
My mother is a Hollywood starlet.
She owns an ark that sits on a high bluff
Overlooking the sparkling Pacific.
I don't like white food, sundials,
Or information off the AP newswire.

I know I'm on a train
Moving through the south of France.
My companion sleeps on my shoulder –
A notebook in her ivory hands.
She has been told to write that we are in love.
There's not a cloud in the sky.

Safe

Lines ache for eyes of freedom.
Before the story of examples we kissed
Through the magnificence of clouds.
I used to guard writing with a frown
And a strong left hand.
In the machine of consciousness
We toil in sentences of regret.
In the dream we were one
And found the scent of vowels on breath
Evoked memory:
I rode a two-wheel bike with
Orange fenders through
A broken timepiece.
The paint in your hair went fantastic.

I've transferred what I know
Into cryptic messages.
We imbibed the given absolutes
Then sunned our bodies on smooth rocks.
I'm an old lizard;
Your passion for technology
Sheds mirrors into star-fed waters.
Hawk in tree feasted on twilight.
Strong verbs gone amuck muck coherence.
There is much to talk about:
Red laces in your black boots
Fragments melancholy.
Let's count something.
Achievement called.

The sketch of shadows in place
Warns conglomerate.
Each of us, each element in us
Flutes improvisation.
Under a dark lamp we fell in love.
I waited in a cosmic field
For a bus, some mode of transportation
That transcended assignment.
Remember freedom;
Remember sculptures of sand
And wave hysteria.
How big are we really?
Release confusion into maps.
I'm here with you.

Swish

Under the umbrella of words
It's a gray day – not without
Laughter.
Switch on the rain.
Rain: it pours off your face
Defining beauty.

I'm far away.
Through the pipes and cranes
Rebuilding the city
Grows the grass of subdued motion.
Walk this field of time:
Speak azalea and hearty rose.

The coffee of luck invades
Our precious conversation.
There's a pen in my hand.
The eye of description filters
A rogue sky.   Recite for me
The commandments of nonsense.

Stalled forest, thin beak, muddy shoes –
I love the reality of naming.
Let's climb a leafless tree.
Listen: a cardinal sings.
Articulate cars on access roads
Flip on their wipers.

And Kiss

1

Horns & beautiful women
Own the streets.
So many of them.
Which one now toots
(Cute)
That I'm hungry –
Have clipped a segment of sky
Into my wallet.
Spirit does not resist sky
& other slogans
In the display windows
Of what everyone needs.

2

The Gallup poll on one more
War is in:
Refuse to tie thoughts
Into knots
Of chemical skin.
Feel the whirling sun.
Spy forsythia in the park.
(Commands…2, 3, 4)
You enjoy being here.
So do others.
The time to live is now
Expresses being.

3

Put away those smart bombs
& buy a fedora or small cigar.
Rehearse Freud (fugue of him)
Ease into the mother love
Left in your brain.
Click on the show of being
Fed by breast.
Discard reptile, oh Federalist!
There is something to protect.
There is something to free.
It's time to walk into a library
& give history a good shake.

4

Expunge the petty need to control
What you control.
Why not if green fish wiggle through you
Whim-wild in delicate hairs of light?
Open up (for Christ's sakes) & smell
The cosmic rose(s)
Bouquet bouquet of fever man.
Each star has a fix on us.
Fix on them.
We all have problems with being.
Some of us – scared & hungry.
Some of us – rich & fat.

5

We all die:
Expecting virgins/
Convinced of light.
Some commit to darkness
& the earth blooms
In the great time it has.
It comes up through the cracks
In sidewalks –
Sneaks birds & whales into memory.
Counting was fun once.
We used to sort and match.
Giggle & kiss.

Statement

I talk about getting old or hug

A tree

It's not raining   the page

Of words you sent me   lingers

But will not reveal

I've reveled once   in the street

With balloons & mermaids

In love with the ocean *of course*

Back to the canopy of leaves

Filed humid & jeweled above my

Head

Huge insect holes   the light

Of the sun   intense

Aging then on the top floor

Of evolution

Without shawl or cane

Time smirks beginning

It's not an engine

An alphabet of molecules takes chance

I just love trees

Sweet Love

1

Big thick text
Crowding the absent
Trees of page

Blue syntax rain gear
In the lovely grass
Of yesterday

Fly into majestic clouds
In a tailspin
Of wristwatch thunderstorms

Like the time
We had the time to discuss
The meaning of time

Everything perfectly rose
Awareness of morning
Bare feet & top hats zooming

Because the story we could tell
Evades us in a parade
Of parking tickets

Because we slump
Under the duties of windshields
& false heavens

2

Let's not walk like ducks
Into the maw of criticism
The logic of senselessness

Plant huge and powerful
Stately & charmed rocks in the thoughts
We have about things

This is a world of small boats
Jewelry socked in opaque pillowcases
Of sweet love

Build variety
Space – gaps (you know) – with adjectives
That mime a plum or jasmine goddess

O the wind of it all
Yawning & sweeping through
Steepled conversations

Everywhere the gods of brick
& sultry hang in the gardens
Of broken sidewalks

Plead with presence & pretense
Salt the eggs
Of textured perceptions

Decision

It starts to rain on a city of bricks.
The next line is imported from Italy.
It's a long and famous line.
Umbrellas open and a man without one
Revisits his childhood.

He plays first base.
He rides on a carousel of painted horses.
He hops from roof to roof
In his neighborhood.
He whispers "symmetry" and rolls in the grass.

He's in love:
A woman rides towards him on a unicycle.
She hands him a line from the next century.
It's about clouds in the sky
Calling his name.

"Over here whale," they say.
"Come quickly parrot," they say.
It is an odd and obscure line.
A little girl laughs.
She loves him and hands him a paper rainbow.

The man thinks:
I'm revisiting my childhood.
I am a child.
His mind is quick and forgiving.
The rain on his lips tastes like licorice.

Out for a drive in their Ford Fairlane
His parents yell out the window at him:
“Blossom,” they scream.
Over and over again: “BLOSSOM!”
He wants to very much.

Go to Oregon

My heels are hot with sand from a Gulf beach.
At night women gamble off beautiful clothes –

Brocades, print dress sunflowers, tads of nothing.
Now is not the time which is an excuse

To mention banana leaf & bougainvillea.
Welcome to the line

& the space after the line.
Experience is past fragmentation.

It's not a partially cloudy sky or even a mix
Of sun & clouds; it's the correct use

Of a semicolon when an angry husband
Calls for a downpour.

Quantum rules if you let it.
So do unnamed insects & aspects of memory.

You were married to an impersonal pronoun.
Regret failed the audition.

You could walk down the street
With an encyclopedia for a friend.

Requisition

I need to buy a pair of skies.
My glasses broke
& yesterday I cried alone
Into the bark of a fat tree.
I love flowers.
The antics of wild fish calm
Submerged highways.
This is a journey of fees & regulations.

The acoustics of the situation remain problematic.
Singers croon in the background of the noisy bar;
The tickle of piano keys tickles apprehensive matrons.
I need to buy a corner lot of your time
To explain my situation.
I didn't get the prophet role.
My investment in burning bushes
Triggered sentence fragments.

I could go on.
My membership in light & the production
Of light is up to date.
I sense the fire in things;
The history of lost time burns like everything else.
I need to buy the essence of emerald
Enjoy a sapphire kiss
Ride the elephant of dawn through screens of consciousness.

This much I know:
The tent of dreams has collapsed;

Clouds are failed actors.
The physics of the situation fizzes
Like antacids in a glass.
I need to buy some comfort, baby!
Come here like you used to
& revive my purchasing power.

Entertainment

Each line has a beauty or humor to it.
Ursula juggled avocados in a dream.

The procession of sentences looks serious.
As a congressman I'd be in a permanent state of ellipsis.

Thank god for lyrical rain.
The old woman slumps through the twilight.

Nothing seems to work.
Acorns bounce off the shed out back.

Out of periods the grammar teacher smiled.
The mind waits sometimes.

Form is a trip.
The Cool Whip is on the door of the refrigerator.

Remember the autumn of knees.
Gold light on the bicycle seat.

Once I brushed my teeth with BENGAY.
It was a time of potholes and pot roasts.

Theories govern the thoughts of the governed.
The red damselfly rose from behind the garbage can.

My neck creaks.
I'll watch the show on giraffes if you do.

Variation on a Field

It's a small space
Like Texas
Or Cupid

You've already written
Your biography
Mom and Dad were pretty

It is dangerous
Someone invented religion
Paths to take

It's OK to fall in love
With a line
Contradict

That outside is inside
Is phenomenally proud
The skein of chair or dilemma

Every move reminds ocean
The horizon of ordinary sings
Death is sacred

We are not lost
In an endless stream
Of mistakes

Composed as chickens
Wheelbarrow collects
Rainwater message

Salutation

Dear friends I'm leaving you for another set of problems.
It was a tough day and the words inside my head
On the nature of reality didn't match yours.
There was the issue of trees; how many salami sandwiches
One could eat during a cloudburst; whether lower case
Letters were upper case ones; were we actually here or not.
We used to have fun: when the ocean was cold and bitter,
When the sun withdrew into dark shadow (refusing dialogue),
We were ready with names, calling names, and swear words
Delivered with such passion – intensity – we surprised ourselves.

Dear friends we were made for sunshine and whim, to walk
Into a convention of lilacs or along a cliff of popped azaleas
(I'm fond of salmon) with nothing in our heads but praise.
We used to run barefoot in the park of romantic inclination.
(You're not hallucinating.) O the kisses we recorded
And shaped into vinyl icons to play like wind in leaves
On the creaky porches of our old age when *kiss*
Had turned to dust in our poor memories and fine complaints.
We had our priorities and called them visions.
For a time we were the rivers, trees, and sky.

Tilt

So you're exhausted!
            The past you knew
Left on a train called
Horizon.
            The sun blazed –
                    Assured of the emptiness
It proclaims.
(A thought)   The
Treasure you want
Evades thought. Shines
Like a full-grown tree –
A child smiling
After a cloud hides a bird
In full flight.
(Obnubilation)
Kingfisher you
Saw in a salt marsh
On a bird walk.
It had a nice haircut.
Claimed it knew Olson –
Hung with him
At postmodern parades.
Signs are events:
Big and looming
At times
Obscuring something
In you.
            Good times
You had with jukebox
And standard religion
Long ago.

Confusion Satori

The bouquet of words in your mind checks for lovers.
You're hurt like the rest of us but refuse to switch to oatmeal
in the morning.
A couplet of roses is not the same or about the same as a
couple of roses.
There are metaphysical questions. Concerns!

Now the narratives of our lives are stored in storage facilities.
Maybe there are a few wild rivers left in a syllable or two.
Proclaim something.
The banjo is waiting for you.

We soar through banal insights into the cabbage of dreams.
Admit to the artwork a good bath permits.
Once you've asked personal pronouns to behave like people
you're in trouble.
Most mechanics refuse to work on misconceptions.

Plead with spontaneity before your pockets fill up with sky.
Fly your hat down the Avenue of Hats.
You could be James Brown.
Uniformity is not the final frontier.

Insight after Dinner at the Diner

I'm not into plot. I hate plot. Give me a sunset any day -
One with lemons, salmon, purple crayons, and aquamarine
Wading pools hidden behind one very long strip-mall.
Anything
But plot. So here's what happened.

I was trapped in Sequence B. It was a small town full of
Closed shoe and cigar factories. Each house composed of
Feathers was blowing away. I yelled to Heloise. "Hey,
Helly, the feather houses are blowing away." "So let them,"
She replied.

I heard the clink of dishes, glasses, and plastic silverware.
A dull clank reminding me of romantic macaroni. Hash in
a can.
I picked up my cigar from the end table. Recited
constellations.
Grew impatient. And recalled the last letter sent to me by
My father.

Dear Son,

I'm heading out to sea. It's infinite out there
You know.

Love,
Sailor Jack

"The pea pod," I said to myself. "The pea pod!" – once or
twice more
In a manner imitating dawn.

Roof and Sky

1

Bird wings & banana trees
In the courtyard of green umbrellas
Word impressions
Throw a dollar bill into the cigar humidor
I'm a fragment
You're a big sack of something:
Wheat flour   pasta   hurricane
The mind balms its injuries
Sunshine hat – you fool

2

Take that the fountain sings through frog-mouth
Cracked slate   &
The haircut cost 18 bucks
Further not farther into the dilemmas of TV
Information fat cats take holiday on sunken boat
On the weathervane of charm –
A nickel's worth of attention
Kiss me with your *shoo* hand
Music we like

3

In the alphabet corner of common sense
Leroy plays his trombone
Agent X arrives from Honolulu
Metallic planes shiver in the metal rain
Again another report of IQ plumbers in the paper

Out of tissues
Lost keys
Rhythm of disjunction flows through feathered brain
Wait time back in ten minutes

4

Imitation harmony distorts the vowel concert
We talked in a complicated way about complex things
Freedom turned into Proposition Secret
Count the votes *damn it* formed government
Exhaust pipes in every pot
Chicken hysteria in the streets
Barkers for sex   Dream
Animal sound asleep
In this way I caught your eye

5

Por Favor
On a rooftop of turistas in the sun
Chewing gum
The shadow of my head on a white page
Blue thunder memory lines somehow
The world in a block highway of words
Cranes build other skies
& the piano player ain't my dad
Honky-tonk stride fingers of pure spirit

6

Contagious text in the heat of false argument
Then a collection of gray buildings for sale
Cars inside radio curlers crawl the streets
Much happiness
& hot sauce to boot on variegated oysters
In time with the tempo
A hat full of Z   Stopwatch
Perceptions near the finish line
So grows the melon of awareness: Iron lace

7

The mystery of each syllable explodes praise
Austrian crystals on a brass string
A shack for consciousness & complaint
Just the other night at the Carousel Bar
We all got dizzy
We must sing
Interstellar message declares the answer
Is a question
Wind across rooftop – gusting beautiful forms

Sound Nets

1

Beef Whiskey and cookies Drink plenty of water
Ignore skeletal aches that come with age
You have a choice Honor something small
Grow into a blue night a man without a hat
a woman igniting a short fuse of happiness
Salt everything Never explain the agendas
of sun and moon Screw toast Being is a word
weighted like dice under the wheels of a tour bus
Numbers aren't significant vegetables Hate
statistics There are green crows (fowl ain't bad
for you) and chemical letters that glow in the dark –
sequence of apples and pears in the veins
mistakes the shape of ribbon candy
virgins on the run

2

Now what does X equal
in the legal sense of deposition that life
sometimes lacks color crackerjack appeal
We talk to ourselves like we're at a filling station
Eventually the teeth of our eyes and fingers made
of fantastic chalk Look our toes are sandy
My how the ocean roars and is our Savior
High ion count Crush of waves Retro
to the present like famous bank robbers
Minds of debarkation construct the birth
and death of stars with new identities
(Solemnly swear) mute nuns and monks
on their way to the beach *gas* silence
Tall ships service the perfect lip of horizon

3

Like clouds of quotidian rain
the mountains of her smile
shadow the time spent
talking about time   Yesterday
my gold watch blinked
on a street of grand hesitation
tuned to the ears of atomic dogs
Gaps then as we've come to denounce them/
pronounce them As if balls of sun in my window gaze
could assuage rules of mind and kingdom
O particle physics and maps of quantum conquests
the sea thunders empathy into dissolving rocks
Free we go into the tympany of sweet equation
whistling out the melancholy   baby

4

The project is incomplete and racing to incompletion
Minus the Cadillac of charm Cubicle 3 whisked
into the room and announced her retirement
Ridiculous – that's not where I was going
A brown envelope of lexical meaning (sealed originally
by jasmine lips) floats in the air like a weather balloon
Yes I love the big yellow sun – hiccups of blue void too
Now when a crocus band loses it on a street of color
what did you expect from hired tambourine handmaidens
Rarely contraindications are fatal
The jalopy of consciousness can run on fumes
shiny apples warts or good luck
Bang the tabletop – the roof of your car
Proceed in the mystery Get out into the country

5

The big bad wolf of holy smoke   primordial
are you shitting me again   dis   clo
sure The girl from the hurricane hesitates
then opens a fabric boutique   Break-out
calypso to freeze the media drool
into scant arabesques   Love baby
crimson dolls of redemption parked
in front of cheap hotels   Maybe
a steak and whiskey or blizzard of delirious
lies in the lens of foolish mistakes with time
There is a need – a greed – for free minds
Inventory of days spent on open seas
Let loneliness chart the steps of starry drunks
on delicate branches

6

More research will buy answers
It's tiny now Don't let it grow up to be painless
Choose the power of window pockets
America's highest yielding bank has changed banks
Coulda   Woulda   Shoulda
Learn Filmmaking
Imagine you're in Tuscany with Andrea Bocelli
You're at risk if you 1. Have no symptoms 2. Wash your hands of information 3. Set new standards for temporary
I've been searching for a church experience for years
Watch your step
Your tax dollars clean up this vehicle
Please remove yourself upon departure
Ask Who What When Where Why Questions

7

Waiting like a dog tethered to an insurance man
Cases of radiant imagination and errant messages
for sale manipulation paltry foreplay
Outside the box of future consequences
spell meadow and false alarm on alpine rocks
Eyes declassified as wide-awake this morning
Flowers absorbed and friendly   articulate nose
No such thing as a stroll to the park or through one
Full out sprint to the batter's box – spike me (me boy)
Whistle of treetops and you're OUT at the plate
Thoughts are raindrop hobos hopping trains
for the seacoast   O the air in your head
like a slate ambulance Blush of thin soul in the blood
unrehearsed   Barking up the wrong security

8

The history of the world invades telecommunications
Think of the iamb before taking a swim
The sky is not made of ceiling tiles
Form is how space exercises
Once a fruit fly dies in the Chardonnay dismantle
the drive-through polis Welcome strangers
Make it new and make it strange
Manifesto pills should be taken every few hours
It's time to ticket the prophet of signs
Once in awhile refers to every day now
Replacement skip the kiss of displacement
Ding-a-ling ding-a-ling ding-a-ling ding-a-ling
Mystery inhabits the woman with blue fingernails
Answer swarms into molecules

9

The orange sky in the sink floats like an airplane
Let's take off this gray day and retrieve
the plastics in the street There's a human shape
to the wind time in a broken clock above the diner
When I order the waitress covers her eyes
with a stick of frogs slips into a trance
Remember the nightgowns mothers laid out for us
The advice crawl on silverware knives and forks
teacups from the interior anyone awake like ants
hop trains inside buildings of condemned towns
I know what it means to lick the night like a stamp
factor in a map of mistakes fake pasture
at dawn and swallow the sun like an aspirin
Come together is the place to water my soul

10

Prophecies rotate in a blaze of swizzle sticks
Compose your appointment with time
We are a nation of rocks
(Tarantulas on imported bananas)
The amount of information is staggering
I have a friend in Paris with 85 francs in his pocket
In a desert of dreams would the phone ring
It was the doctor who said *Go ahead and fart*
We are now free to make up our names
In line at the random word machine
when you said *Pass me the loneliness*
I write in a time of profound tragedy
Preposterous
Like memory in the forest of self

11

From Galileo's balcony things are falling
Say with me *verde verdant verdure*
Sip the chicken soup and tell the waitress
I'm ready to walk right out of my head
If pen moves there is motion
If dogs bark it's not one of those days –
uptight angels edgy for cloudless bodies
You know what I mean –
bewildered creatures drinking mint juleps
mouths shut on sky Yes let's order
another soup d' jour with saltine crackers
Green helicopters chart our position
When I say *Where to*
Let's get the hell out of here

12

Boat of blond strangers has too many opinions
Time to float   Current of thought
less than Nile but not my exotic mother
Like the sun inside a letter she was incomprehensible –
a veiled dance of water and minerals
Take Rembrandt (for instance)
the fit of new slippers the history of sleep
in a small box of freeways and telekinetic balloons
self as an episode of Italian waiters singing
like a penchant for rare books   Just walk
into a bar convenience store shopping mall
Whale and chair don't belong in the same sentence
Yo Ishmael
The tragedy of love is still love

13

I remained incognito during most of this
In Tibet via a simple telepathic wish
It was a simple venture – anything anyone
wanted could be tossed against his or her house
in the middle of the night in a waterproof box
Just found out his dot.com venture tanked
No siree   rolling back and forth in the yard
has nothing to do with Enlightenment
Chuzang-Tsu hopped down streets on a single foot
Maya seems like a beautiful curtain
(with only a slight tear)
In conversations on fate gesticulate wildly
Who said cricket symphony this time of year
Former lives and duties

14

Bridge gap Ulysses
Conversation claimed tattoos of rose
Broken dawn emits enough light
to embark on a sea of sibilant words
It's about words
Speed   whims
beyond telecommunication
systems   Full of cause and notions
dreams nurture them
into oracles of perfect vision
In the tantrums of kiss and deep embrace
(hot Romantic) they attend thought
They *gotta* head somewhere
Hoist signs for nothingness and journey

UNDER THE SKY OF NO COMPLAINT

Complete Thought

Someone shouts   the architecture of brainwave technology
I'd rather listen to dogs barking
Fireworks and wind
Through summer screens
Then complete a thought   A sentence is a complete
Thought   A new sentence is a completely new thought
Instead of signs and signifiers everyone is mad at me
I said *artifice* for the hell of it
Reinstated the humidity in conversation
After a downpour
    Look something made
    An uncapped pen on my maple desk
    Hesitate then proceed
    To record last night's discussion
    Between two stones
Yes   your eyes were tropically red
Yes   I misplaced my allegory in the bus station
Yes   there were an old man and woman wearing striped
        Bandannas
      Sawing   an   ocean
          Plank
      In   two
I whispered *mockery of lips*
    And took a chance
    The pirate of abstraction
    Knew how
    To pastel the sea
O sometimes I see them at their desks clapping their hands
At the pace of words

Across shimmering deserts   According to one
    report
Journalists with belts are beating the news
Another states diet pills hasten immortality
    I'm as current as the day lilies
    On my street
    Subscribing as I do
    To *Flower Jazz*
Yes   the moon in the sky   that's all
                                        And curtains billowing
Messages of welcome

Origin

To impress you I've walked on
Waters of dissonance
Clouds make their own wine now
& my takeout orders stay hot
Fish in the street remain nameless
& multiply by indirection
If it's time to wait
Call me – if not the dance of continents
Appears extreme   Once upon a snowball…
Once upon every extinction report or impulse
Please help us therapists cry
As children brave elements of now
Hydrogen started it
After that it was a sitcom of trial & error
But here we are with sweeter music &
Magnificent examples of digitized consciousness
I wish you could understand me
If only letters still existed
I would write one that invented love
The moment we met

Under the Sky of No Complaint

The traffic looks bad
And the jets overhead fade into consciousness

I have a message to someone somewhere
And cell phone numbers on slips of paper in my wallet

I could have been a Romantic or enjoyed
The spontaneity of spontaneous verse in the absence

Of salons on my street
Which means

I'm a nobody in love with flowers of dawn
And the mixed metaphors of another day

Why the hell not
The School of Advanced Poetics has stalled

In mid-sentence and the clean metaphors
Of what may have taken place

Have been dredged like an obsolete sea
Meaning of course or foretelling

For those in hermeneutic boots
Something else than what was intended

And because I'm a fan of the moon
And the word *aletheia*

I've taken the AP course on writing
On *Return to Sender* envelopes

In particular the sealed flap –
Loose as the anger inside of me

And lost in a seam of time
Like a trilobite

Empty Mailbox

for W.E. Butts

Hemlocks flail in square windowpanes of light
I'm writing a letter to myself
It reads like a grocery list
Dear Memory
I could use an avocado
A bag of chips
Stuff like that
Plus
The lack of winter storms entertains my mind
Like white wine
Pears
And cheese
Later
I might write
In paragraph two of the body
(If I remember to indent)
    The hip pocket version of my past will do for now
We all had bikes and bibles
Air-raid drills and surgically implanted doubt
I never suffered a meltdown or Navy tattoo
Though dad's brimstone lips ignited my mind
The day the ocean arrived on our doorstep
As a catalog of unsigned dreams
Remember
Dear Past
The world is not a foolish sequence of timed-out events
The droopy petals of a family of irises crop my attention

When I garden in a trance of now
The nectar of words tempts hummingbirds
Night flows from the pen too
A halo of black holes subsumes religious icons
The letter ends when it stops
If it has
Yours truly
Will or did I receive it

I Do

Start with a blank universe
On a blank page It's cold outside
And it would be foolish to answer emails
That inquire if you exist or not Of
Course you have memories There was
The time you could start…mention
Baseballs or kisses beneath the apple
Tree Or how this morning you claimed
Maybe even exclaimed into a bowl
Of Cheerios that Eve (as mother) a mere
Nanosecond ago bit the fruit and started
Our trek into visibility It's basically
How the brain feels or perhaps the will
Or even the soul You know that you're
Writing and fantasize that another treatise (on
Anything) would be just the right thing now
Like it's so incredibly instantaneous and
Disturbing We don't get along and
Seem to enjoy talking over this fact
As in the following example *My god is*
Blue and belongs to the hierarchy of
Clouds and tremendous raindrops while
Yours is into statistics and once
Claimed the bell
Curve of stars rings
Like the ears of
A strange inventor
Yes we all love
The particles of our

Intense fabric and
Given the news
We could lapse
Into a trance
Of appropriate
Forgetfulness
So now then
As we often say
To each other
Before tying shoes
And heading out
Into the buzz
Of adroit sequence
Do you love me or not

The Garden of Upside-Down Trees

for Dave Brinks

So brave your heart
Running from the authorities suited you
Past memory and the full contact gear of the present
Who sings sweetly to me now

I've done the math
The archaic maestro of abstruse conversation
Stuck his tongue out at me
Trumpets bent their notes

Mental equations for childhood didn't work
The time to invoke a phenomenological reduction
On the contrite beauty of raindrops
Had passed

Given the status of my green card
It was cold in the barrio without thermostat
Or topological map
I was not the future of the heart's revolution

Granted this was a rough cut
As I recall you crushed a cigarette under foot
Before the chandelier of morning
Crashed to the floor

I thought of that-you thought of that
The mystery of dawn shuddered
After Einstein dropped Newton
Into the maw of gravity

Furiously
I thumbed through fibrous pages of empty space
Until the attack of gumball machines
Entered the fray of neophyte sentences

No kidding my feet itched
But did the holistic therapist need to lower
Cough drops into an imaginary fish tank
When the pilot announced his solo flight

Within range of a thunderclap of lips
The smokestack of ideas collapsed
Into the alphabet soup
Then we drove into a river of moons

I became a dilettante of unrest
Now draw the ellipsis of chance
And waters of neglect to scale
The house band told me

The hysterical addiction of consciousness
To the antics of information fractals
(Like spoiled children in a vat of 3D glasses)
Blew the mind of the JumboTron

Under a hurricane of pissed off street lamps
The parrot in the audio track of dreams
Disclosed the purpose of writing
Once inside a particle accelerator

Meanwhile the Maelstrom of Ceremony
Stole the architectural plans
For a casually caused universe
From the Guru of Indeterminacy

I turned off the light and scrolled through darkness
Outside the wall of doors
The Garden of Upside-Down Trees
Floated by

Subtle Difference

The flock of ancestral birds
In my eyes
Is not the same
As the gang of metaphors
In yours

Inside the tent of trees
Rain howls

After Prosody Class

I'm a connoisseur of weather balloons
Sorghum is my favorite
Followed by metaphysics and St. Paul
Sometimes things go awry
In a line of poetry
A tornado hits
Instead of the speed of light
Or a peach cast from a branch
Of thin air

Silence reigns
The ocean is a velveteen quilt
A band member with a broken guitar string
The mailbox suffers an empty stomach of sound
It's time to wait at a red light
For a basket of groceries
Missionaries at the front door
With pamphlets on Presence
Read absent lips

If the past intrudes
Father was a grand mal gangster
Mom played the piano for pleasure
Are lines to scan
Of course there are gaps to consider –
Nights of stressed and unstressed lovers
With hummingbird tattoos
The pattern of grease from a bicycle chain
On a pair of hands

The poem is always about something else
It has a history –
Was a track star at Mineola Prep
Sold electromagnetic fields
Door to door
As well as insurance
Maybe it's the Declaration of Independence
Or the United States Constitution
It detests the strip search

Eventually there is a tower of rocks
In the backyard
Without a metaphor in sight
A visiting archaeologist produces notepad and spade
There is work to be done –
Artifacts and archetypes to plunder
"Watch for gas lines," I shout
Before blue jays in the hemlocks
Steal breakfast

Stoic Surrender

Time chisels its self-portrait
In an outcrop of rocks
Above a blue highway
It's a night of bugs
Chilled fireflies ships of silence
Flickering memories
And the feet ache
Under the influence of women
And red wine
I write by candlelight

Let's agree on the multiplicity
Of place choice and dilemma –
The need for fabrication
In institutions of brittle reason
Should I lie about youth –
The rate of vaporization
In the geological Yin/Yang
The melt-rate in the heart of love
I was banned from Alexander's great library
Before it burned to the ground

My teeth flash smoke signals
A willow branch mimes the swan's neck
I love you like temperature –
Whisper Celsius to buttons on your blouse
Under a regime of polar instructions
Snowflakes issue the commands
Memory is a reliable portfolio
Kiss me green eyes
"Run, horses, run!" I cry
Cars pass by

Elegy

It's no secret that the mind is troubled

In school Harry studied nuclear metaphysics and watched violent cartoons

This is a prose poem

Jane got upset when the librarian told her the *History of Spirit, Vol. 3*

Was never returned

Through the nineties most consumers drifted through an ahistorical maze

Of stock options and virtual promises

Then history returned

Grief and fear were palpable

Some scrambled to re-read the prophecies of wild-eyed prophets

Others fell on their knees and realized the stars above their heads

Were real and beautiful

This is a diary –

A place for words to mourn

Each of us is a young child running to the park to play

Now say this

We've been ambushed

The silver and bronze of dreams weep gold

This is a science report

Our genes are bad

Space is finite

Deep in the pockets of nothing run the wild rivers of cause and effect

Once upon on a time we told magnificent stories about gravity and galaxies –

Considered awareness more than a ripple of wind across a pond

Of somnolent fish

We knew how to count by the billions and billions of years

we were not here

This is a letter

Dear Friends

Dear World

Our penchant for death is ridiculous

Yellow Tulips

Fatigue sets in
Like a broken watch
On a crumbling mountaintop

Words
Do their
Homework

The plain horse
Of synapse
Coughs

Beyond number
The sky recedes into a bank
Of yellow tulips

Tattered Soliloquy

It was more of an allegiance to indigo than twilight that
allowed vertical bars of paint to access the unknown

We all wore watches back then and feigned an allergy to
lemon trees

To compose was to become lost in the act of composition

Green leafy vegetables and broken hearts came together as
a set of equations that either advanced civilization or laid
the foundation for roads to nowhere

It was a complex haven of tax shelters that everyone knew
something about

Antecedents the final magician of decadence mumbled into a
fashionable hat

I wanted very much to wander in the aquamarine fog behind
my eyelids and so I did

I'm sorry for transgressions mystical states of mind and buying
religious accoutrements at a going out of business sale

Chastising chastity worked well as a calling card before the
sunset of love

Who said the world has fallen into a vortex of doldrums

There is something in the soul equivalent to the genome of
    joy in a basket of flowers or an erotic kiss

We struggled to keep up with an expanding universe

I deferred to multiple takes on logos during lunar holidays
    and solar flares

The absolute brilliance of the absolute is what we continually
    tried to articulate to one another   relatively speaking

The blues of persuasion assuaged the gaudy mechanism of
    chance operations

I built salt flats of excess baggage on the outskirts of social
    media for a reason that now escapes me

I remained a fresh water animal in a blaze of deserted deserts

The crows in my yard forgot to caw goodbye

The Pleasure of Noticing

1

The café of sad women redeems hairdos
I lost my glasses in moonlight
& the next day went to the bank
To complain Full of allegory
I could've used a getaway car
Or a shine on my shoes For
The sake of irrelevance I maintain
A constant hello

2

I sold my hair at a garage sale
If I say I love chopped liver
My addiction to a lyrical
Narrative ego could go unnoticed
The last string of words
To invade my space caused
Some hilarity though neighbors
Called the cops

Promontory Scrum

1

Response succumbs to
Intimidation and regret
I knew you in the salt mines
Of hope I could hardly
Wait to foster incoherence
After the news cycle
Left me alone There were
The Aeneid to consider
Horrendous misspellings
The beauty of a shower
With a beautiful woman
And the canned laughter of
Clergy

2

I became a man during
The hostile takeover by adjectives
The Big language Bosses bought
The field of dreams and busted
Teeth
The heavens issued
An encyclical
On particles and
Dust The last
Supernova in the eyes
Of unbelievers
Took root in
The quotidian shakedown

3

It's OK to wait
For the changing of the guard
Each word in the alphabet of euphoria
Has passed out I know what
You want on your violent screens
Of distraction Evolution
Seeps through the bloodstream
And smiles pure innovation
Dance with me
In the sexual haze
Of distance or I will
Count to 100
And hold my breath

4

I hear the sirens of dreams
In your hesitation to know me
I'm the author
Foot soldier
Menace
Clown
What could these possibly mean
In an era of silent lips
And sullen eyes Lead
Me onto a beach of stranded
Dolphins Consider reconciliation
On the proverbial
Hill of beans

Spaced Remarks

I have fallen asleep in the grape of afternoon

I have forgotten my name

But will watch ideas in my head jump from a bridge

Parachutes I think

Or the sounds of war into oblivion

I'm here to record

Like yellow tiger lilies I favor composition

Without mirrors

As in full summer or distraction

The drum of meaning is more than silent

Like moon

Symbol

A detached retina

Before remembering the humid barks of dogs

Or midnight traffic

It's tough to love so much

To ache like the irregular beat of seasons

In the heart

*

We need to know that we are bigger than our small complaints

Today I won't answer the phone

Fear TV

Or respond to emails with a treasure chest of Band-Aids

And interrupted storylines

In other words I'm unavailable

Or simply that forgery of misunderstood questions

In the mind like a grove of orange trees

Struck by lightning

Squeeze me

I'm that kind of association

*

While in the temple of rhythm edit the duty roster

That's you (or me) in your car –

A loud river coursing not cursing through nerves

Like the sudden absence of what was present

It's OK to shout

I guess I'm spontaneous

As in the way you or I talk to our selves

In a world made of stars and aging

While tapping steering wheel

Glaring through windshield

We've got the beat   animal

We're human after all

Before Dawn

Birds are part of it
Chirping in trees
Before the sun rises

Being is not a dream
Being dreams the language
Of the mind

Let the dog bark
The ceiling fan
Hums cool air

Wait
Pause
Refuse time

The vast beauty of space
Absorbs turmoil
Creates it (just a thought)

Now trumps myth
But myth counts
The psyche is older than we are

Message inserted Rise
Stir wind (toss trees)
Feel fine

Doused with angels
Free words
Fly

I've been in love
A dozen times or so
It seems

Retroactive

1

Here we are on TV
In the fantasies of yesterday

Once I smashed guitars
And burned draft cards

Then got married
Sure I like whiskey

And immediate gratification
Let's wear tie-dyed t-shirts

Under the pink champagne
Of stars

2

Too bad I didn't graduate
From Princeton

Or adopt a postmodern haircut
We're cute and clever now

In the absence of history
Instantaneous messages

Tell us to fuck off
Or get to work

Still we wait
Deep in our hearts

The beauty of aesthetics lurks
Like a criminal

3

We live on automatic pilot
And shop at Home Depot

Just the motion of a critical pen
Clears the proverbially bar (room)

Mere fantasy
As media consultants form

In single file
Behind gross celebrities

4

There used to be farms
And farm animals

Days we wandered in black-eyed Susan
Free of our time bruise

How collaged can we become
So we wait

In the predicted charms
Of the unexpected

I love you
You know that

Strip Meditation

1

Chair of time
Dream hair reported to civilian authorities
Blue laced with gray
By the time the lagoon shrank
Invariably specialty drinks
Under an umbrella of black silk

Refreshment fantasy
Prism of pelicans in tight formation
Mushroom of remembered sky
Under the influence we played all day
Light the chauffeur for your immense
& pleasant beauty

2

The first line of moon is defense
Calendar of international events
Complains time
Vibrations are free
Or feverish
Steps of desire within words

The bigger picture of beauty
Ring of truth in the ears
Decisions linger in memos & dust
Documentation counts
Research flexibility
A black moth rests on green grass

3

It's not a question of intelligence
Flowers fold into themselves
During thunderstorms
Knowing when to pause

The point of not coming to the point
Has to do with the rearrangement
Of what we perceive in front of us
Like a bus

The melting point of iron in the mother dust cloud
Was low enough to establish a core
Line by line
Language tolerates the mind's confusion

We are here
Grain accretions of temporality
& because it's summer the ice cream truck
Trundles through the neighborhood

4

Narrative sunset in your eyes
As gift
Leaves blew down the street
In a sailor of wind
Voyage of color and sound

Boundaries of sea & wet syllables
We whistled intention to each other
Like dolphins
In the belly of a dream
Called story

5

Because it has stomped around
Jumped high & off reasonable roofs
The body is resistant to flight

(Remember
We kissed in a field
Of yellow flowers)

Each day we get to…
Must talk with others –
Things are not right

Too much work
Many problems
Not enough time

We praise animals
They sleep in the sun
& offer blank eyes

We're empty
The mind is a movie screen
Without audience

Fingers filter sky
Clouds tethered to words
Fly by

6

Heroes dot the landscape
Clocks remain permanently unfixed
Don't touch my syntax
Trees weep
Double-parked Cadillac on Destination Ave.

Soaring sweet sounding clouds
In the physicists' pockets: Cubist symmetries
& strings of Proper Names
Without claiming X
Beautiful women mother exciting times

So epochs of memory the size of marbles
The ocean in you for a day
In front of the liquor store pansies in concrete beds
Imaginary steps concealed in the workout
Solid forms

7

One mind leaps from the past
To the present
Another doesn't

The future is a big dot
Somewhere in the neighborhood
Of no sky

How could that be
Be is just that –
What we do

Planes fly over my words
Yellow jackets orbit my house
Let me speak like the wind

It is soft & comforting
Today
I'm in love with it

Tie what together
Yield to space
Visit a quantum delicatessen

We all go on
Run-on like sentences
Down the street

They must be flags
These subjects & predicates
O tectonic mind slips

8

1

Snow on the hemlocks
Thought is motion
Outside the barn of stars a tired self
Puffs on a cigarette
The wind howls a tune of perfect ice
Memories leave the church of language in single file
My heart like metaphor needs something

2

Is there a miner of interpretation in the house
I'm not lost or buried under a black sky
Send me a batch of words from where you are
That we miss each other feigns tautology & neglect
I am here in the journey of light like I told you
My eyes are green & into swans
Quiet now   time has never ticked

9

A word forgets it's a word
& becomes the sky a leaf
Memory shard or dream fragment
The sky is full of words for itself
Now open to moods
Of blue turmoil & light
As an avenue of space –
Pristine canvas unencumbered
By history heroes malaise
Or insight before drifting
Into a stream of words
Similar to consciousness
& what's occurred

10

The sky looks down on memories in a red cage

The highway through the first dream branched into a hemlock forest

Through bitter tears (it looks like) hope has disappeared

Is it connected to magic

Bring forth multifarious birds in furious displays

I have wings There must be wings

Rock

Externalizing mind into sounds of pen

Practice thinking

You'll have to wait until tomorrow

11

Start with distraction
As the impression
Memory of fog
The moment you
Entered it
You can't

Dictate people
But there are
Many around you
Enjoying themselves
Drinking beer
& telling stories

Of course the women
Are beautiful
Exchanging
Conch shells
For pearl clocks
Without numbers

Squint again
Into the light
Of a smeared moon
The story
On your lips
Is about trees

Your manner
Of walking
Through them
As mind
Builds a bridge
In the mist of meaning

12

Thoughts turn into sentient rivers
We lived in trees for a time
Grew our love of sky from there

The simple repetition of tears & names
Indigo sheep ignore the moon
Thanks to impulse self whittles vision

Things to say about the world
The well is deep
It's time to bend the shallow knee

13

The ache to comprehend grew sullen
It was not the time to write

Outside the sun was hot
& foreign

Dogs in a morning chorus of hibiscus
Barked at trilling birds

Which ones he didn't know
Having inserted himself like a flaming coin

Into the silver moment
There were clouds in the sky

Piled on top of each other
Like the maimed hats of a French designer

In storage now
In a country of beautiful rivers

Gorgeous as the space available
To anyone with wings

14

In time we will
Overcome everything

If we are the immense universe
& not some egomaniacal

Splinter of light in the mind
Then we'll arrive

On a barge of feathers
At the source

Of our musical proclivities
(The present not the future

Vibrates in a symphony
Of unrehearsed moments)

As dawn sings an aria
For the unseen

Wake up & play
In beats of light

Skylark

In the Bag

The big bag of words landed inside his head
Like an alien spaceship So many lights
And with such great commotion he concen-
Trated on the moment when he would use
The words to reinforce his claim that
Language was an inexhaustible playhouse
Of sounds and didn't mind a single bit
Those who warred about forms and con-
Straints and/or wild freedom in order
To compose a thought an emotion or world
Consider any words in the bag their his-
Tories proclivities possible arrange-
Ments in space Take *rinse cycle* for
Example For him it meant to dance down
The street in the middle of a thunder-
Storm ignoring the horns of cars or the
Cries from passengers to expunge himself
From the galloping raindrops and return
At once to his washing machine or dish-
Washer to await the correct sequence of
Buzzers to finish his assigned household
Chores He was home after all free from
The workplace due to a glitch in the fed-
Eral computer that inappropriately la-
Beled him an anarchist in spirit and
Prone to long periods of morose doubt
About the acuity of his intellect when it
Came to summing numbers Or how about
The word *trellis* A word that literally

Poked up and through the bag and for him
(And he will argue with you about this
Deep into the night) was there for a vine
Of syllables to wind its way silly and
Beautiful as a river of roses – the one
That looked so good clinging to our old
Farmhouse before strong winds from the
Temperamental sea blew in

Ice Cube Cantata

Orthographic rules succumb to the demands
Of angry spelling bee contestants
The country as in the new polis of yesterday's nightmare
Beats the hell out of the chill in a lover's eyes
Language wants to dance – Hoedown to Motown
Hello to the myth of being here or not

I had a secretary once who bet the horses
And offered me the fetlock of her spirit
Sensei you say
With a guffaw and a kick in the butt
This is not the proper venue to discuss whether
Poetry should be doggie paddle accessible or not

Bile Inc. was the previous appellation
Of my flirtation with a small business
As an American strapped to the Autonomous Complaint Factory
Of Notoriously Ineffective Legislators
I must say (as Ned said)
Put us all back to work you insufferable assholes

I still appreciate the Moody Blues and mushroom parties for the elderly
The content of consciousness flows into the spillway of tomorrow
I knew from the start of the Big Bang
Issues would surface in the radar of whatnot
Lexical minds remain skeptical of assisted-living facilities
For contrarian conversations

Multiple Agendas in the Concept of One

On the verge of collapse
The psyche pitches out of it
Human commodities woo the public
In a hail of modifiers sentence police
Burst through the front door

An unknown countenance frames the sky
Physics dreams the final equation
As for the impish distraction of time
While laughing oranges
We made a documentary on love

I'm used to lips as bouquets of flowers
The self is a cocktail party
Beyond the intrusion of dark matter
Or a construct of elusive variables
Penny candy stores resume normal operations

In the hum of rivers and lakes
Your body reflects mine
We peal the calendar of days
In a maze of language games
False statements return to the server

Euphoria

The organism of mind needs the sea and endless sky
Blue flowers of hope eschew simple delivery
I'm not on a plane or an astronaut with tools
The alphabet has come to town like a missing person

It's not raining sentences of nonsense
A veil of clouds with a terrific thirst for land
Has transformed subtle kites into circus animals
The harbor of regret is not for you

Ring the doorbell
I'm home in digital silence with a flask of whiskey
We were once in a parade which banned flags
And multisyllabic disorders

Within a decade the general populace
Will be able to take mandolin lessons on the moon
Newshounds provide imprecise information
Cut loose on the lonely page as self

Swoon if you must in a mirror of perpetual motion
I'm in love and find it difficult to find shoes that fit
Bubble in test answers about Beethoven with #2 pencils
We want to make sense but don't have to

The mind digs corrective action
Stocks float off shore with executives and mermaids –
In deeper water fish like chess and backgammon
Choose your fate

Light requires one to account for missing keys
Just say I'm as happy as sunshine
Before it rains on enchantment install new locks
Don't compete with the precipice of time

Syllable Town

A weed in the central metaphor
Church bells ring

Rules for line
Break off
Into sea

Clap hands to turn on lights
Rubber legs
For rubber mountains

Whispering *daisy*
A trucker tests his brakes

Plummeting
Down
Steep
Grades

Mayhem Interlude

The hybrid of beauty walked down the street with a gold
dog
All the adjectives in the China mines of yesterday shivered
into a cold sweat
A tsunami of opportunity broke loose in the neighborhood
as the sun set
A few wet souls went for a swim in a fading stream
Trees whispered to each other while the moon cued in &
out of clouds –
A smudge of chalk dust on its trombone face like a blue
pimple

It was time to howl or invest in stocks
Perfect strangers dropped cell phones into garbage
receptacles
Hustling into parallel lines of wireless intuitions
First they blew kisses to each other – kisses that preferred a
kingdom of fans
& balsam airplanes for stylistic landings on cheeks &
foreheads
So what if the lips were missed
Deep in the desert of their listening (# 2 by the way) they
heard
Imaginary coyotes of longing gather by the ruby rock of true
wealth

The hybrid of beauty paid no attention
It was time for the world to grow up to what it was & where
it was going

O the gold dog had some thoughts on the matter
The advancement of sidewalks it thought
In the good old days of Swiss watchmaking it pondered
When sparkling coins of disconnected rain struck the street
 it seemed a shame
Like something preplanned & controlled by a band of gypsy
 clichés
Could the gold dog relate – embrace faux liquidity
As for the proverbial parade the hybrid of beauty opened
 an electric umbrella

Closure in a Time of Complaint

The streams of love are statements now
Events of language and dawn fused like song
In the house of semiotics

Forget the metaphor of place
Rock has retired
Escape into the Academy of Dreams

Let me shake your hand
It's a vast conspiracy of time and duty
Wouldn't you say

Gold flaring tongues explode into space
The miniscule history and behavior of hydrogen
The universe is a business

But something else
Something constructed with
All the effort due meaning

Beauty affects the brain
Phrase of lakes or demented suffering
In a vast fabric of brilliant equations

Crew cut of wax and neighborhood
I froze at bat
Took one in the nuts for the team

Thump

Don't inhale

-

The history of color

-

Has lapsed

-

Into conflict

-

Once tall as a tree

-

The subject

-

Exudes forgetfulness

-

Of illusion

-

Words are

-

Sentinels of laughter

-

In the poker hand

-

Of association

-

Say something

-

Hierarchy had an idea

-

Of itself

-

As a replicable pattern

-

Now is the moment

-

For some splendid

-

Gymnastics

-

To exercise like clouds

-

Fall onto the page

-

As rain

-

Disassociation is the same

-

Type of game

-

Beauty is each

-

& every one of us

-

Kiss as flowers do

-

Yell sand

-

Sing melodic

-

Embryo of tomorrow

-

Electric shoeshine man

-

Thump

Talking Heads on Mute

Media is a gall bladder attack
And after the installation of deliberate falsehoods
Will fully recover
Horizontal dreams perpetuate opinion polls
So we wait

News by constant video clip
The world is here (outside the window)
Sing Ava Maria
Mirrors lost in the swan of shadows reflect transcendence
So much for brilliance

On the summit of discontent
The jukebox of chance cues
The heartstrings of lost minutes
I was young and into flowers
Let's do chocolate

Reports so far are a series of random thoughts
Playing tag at Ground Zero
Language rises from the dead
O snail of sentences which way went thy narrative
Like a somnolent figment of imagination

The sky forever with us
Promotes an erudite friendship
With clouds we should emulate
Now back to the truth
Yes

Semantic Arteries

Words are too heavy
They've grown fat
With centuries and mouths

Any one of them
Could flatten any one of us
Like a railroad penny

Go ahead
Lie down on their tracks
And see what I mean

Fame

for Joel Dailey

1

The reviews on the
Refrigerator are chilled
And alone The television
Is on and the sanity
Test has been filled
Out in triplicate
I wrote the book
Which exposed the
Excesses of excessiveness
The beginning of nation
States delineated
Plummeting
Gravity

2

I've dated falsettos
And once was
Fooled by falsies
During a tractor pull
The requirement to
Remain astute dims
In coherent darkness
I've heard
A staccato of words
Assault false horizons
My uncle gave me
A ukulele and a kick
In the ass

3

The advancement
Of civilization depends
On identity theft
And downloaded
Movie stars
I love the geometry
Of an eviction notice
Addressed to foreboding
Mind swings and sheds
Interference to enter
The fame-free zone of enlightenment
Grow still as contradiction
In a plethora of sunsets

4

I'm lost in the headlines
Of my face in the mirror
America has *it*
And the media of
What went right
Is under house arrest
I practice the scales
On my back and stay
Loyal to the dictates
Of effusive attention
Would you prefer my solo
In a minor key or a portrait
Of simple decline

Bullets

- On a lost page of sun
- In the found universe
- Conversations with virtual women
- Ruffle the leaves of trees
- Splash of concrete shadows
- Time to pass out scale models of moon and stars
- Once upon a time
- Twice in no time
- Like when you have a high temperature or break out in a rash
- Ink on the hands is warm and bubbly
- Everything counts
- Mind is metaphor
- Everything discounted
- Ignore the voyeur floating through the text
- Earth and its inhabitants are traveling through
- The Scorpius Centurius connection
- Digress when language wants to
- Phenomena so small there's no technological equipment to measure them
- Pen as waterfall or saxophone
- Prospect of shagging flies under a perfect sky
- Varied scarves of wind
- Oops
- Over we go in the vortex boat
- Who recalls their days as pelicans
- Gliding above slate waves

- In jet fighter formation
- The path of comets through Enlightenment
- Free floating words: collision dregs microbe oblivion
- No tags or qualifiers placed on omnipresence
- Eyes rinsed with compassion

Title

Whether "faith" or
Not
Is part of
The religious experience

A satchel of rivers
A satchel of river
Poems

Stone steps
The wisdom tree
Shouting omnipresence
Into a crowd

The number of interpretations
Possible
Meaning cowering in fear

Momentary wait
Rereading the event
Of words

Who's guiding the unknown hand
The sex of it
Deep in the bones

All those flowers
And kids
The upright walk
Attributed
To the clown of happiness

Splash some art
On it
Unfurl magic commandments

Consider the
Act of construction
The stapler
On the desk
Arrangement of scattered
Pens
And pencils

Postcards of
Encouragement
Surround you
Say nothing

(In the
Parenthesis)

Romantic train
Whistles
In the distance

Slip Up

I've forgotten my role in the mystery of things
There were times of sipping whiskey
The color of sky and sudden rainfalls
I felt good on macadam and spent holidays
Beside the eruptions of manhole covers
I was a man of polis and charm and could linger
In the past of what I said or refused to say
After all was just a favorite transition
To a baseball game or the memory
Of an ex-lover with choice things to say
To the new lover about my multiple failings
I was OK in terms of corrals
But after that it was a dissertation on bad haircuts
Present temperature and the latest insight
On the purpose of applause
I was a character trait teetering on a period gone bad
I feigned the openness expected
In the company of IQ charts and dilemmas
I claimed to have stopped while driving through
The barriers of what was next

Skylark

1

Tiny poems belong
On tiny slips of paper
The moon is a tiny
Slip of paper

Good morning blue sky
There are no line breaks
Even in the clouds
You propose

Green vowel spontaneity
On a day home from work
She looks into the Martian
Of my eyes

Violets you say
And then you say violets
What of the violets you say
About the violets

The habit of pink
Strolls into view
This is a note of depth and beauty
It is pink

Gray thoughts
Travel like whales

Into pure destination
We swim among them

It is not either/or
Nor black and white
Contrast is nuance
Not nuisance

2

Vision is often noisy
And quite distracted
If we are one
Hold off on answering the next email

Under the constellations of heaven
There are plenty of options
Instead of forests we could have
More superhighways (for instance)

Witness the cellar of oranges
Climb lemon steps at the sun's request
Squeeze the light in you
Into shapes of day

After the sobriety test
Comes the test for celebrity
In a month all the shoes in the kingdom
Will be assessed

Once we throw out method

We'll land on *The Isle*
Of Flat Stones…
And skip them

The mind waits
Then calls for a taxi
The taxi arrives
And it's time for a cigar

The brittle fact of your voice
On the day a skylark
Auditions songs of flight
Sings to me now

3

Into words until trees known
And lips kissed
Are not moon or blue complaints
We're pissed at something

The politics of periods
Sessions of pause and history
Rocks came before
The dust of love

The tools of perception
Praise sunrise
One full day of flowers
In rudderless wind

It's time to get up
Retrieve mysteries outside the window
Laundry on the line
The memory of shouting

Claim voice as soliloquy
Expose the gestures of pure sound
You're a wave
Frequent roots and ideas

Become still as illusion
Oak leaves or gravity
Somersault mornings of feeling fine
Light your hypnotist

File work under the compulsion
To frolic in freedom
We're together in the dictionary
Of subtle glances

About the Author

Richard Martin is the author of *Dream of Long Headdresses: Poems from a Thousand Hospitals* (Signpost Press, 1988), *White Man Appears on Southern California Beach* (Bottom Fish Press, 1991), *Modulations* (Asylum Arts, 1998), *Marks* (Asylum Arts, 2002), *boink!* (Lavender Ink, 2005), and *Altercations in the Quiet Car* (Fell Swoop/Lavender Ink, 2011). Martin is a past recipient of a National Endowment for the Arts Literature Fellowship for Poetry and the Honorary Poet Laureate of Binghamton, NY. He lives in Boston with his family

19090630R00090

Made in the USA
Charleston, SC
06 May 2013